PORTRAIT OF
THE SHROPSHIRE HILLS

ROBIN JUKES-HUGHES

HALSGROVE

First published in Great Britain in 2009, reprinted 2012

Copyright © Robin Jukes-Hughes 2009

British Library Cataloguing-in-Publication Data
A CIP record for this title is available from the British Library

ISBN 978 1 84114 936 3

HALSGROVE
Halsgrove House,
Ryelands Business Park,
Bagley Road, Wellington, Somerset TA21 9PZ
Tel: 01823 653777   Fax: 01823 216796
email: sales@halsgrove.com

Part of the Halsgrove group of companies
Information on all Halsgrove titles is available at: www.halsgrove.com

Printed and bound in China by Everbest Printing Co Ltd

INTRODUCTION

AN AREA OF OUTSTANDING NATURAL BEAUTY

In 1958 the Shropshire Hills became one of the first parts of England and Wales to be designated an 'Area of Outstanding Natural Beauty' (AONB), and they remain to this day one of the most beautiful, tranquil and unspoilt parts of the country. They have been a popular holiday destination since Victorian times and now attract over half a million visitors a year. But if you get away from the popular valleys and hiking trails, you may not see another person all day. The aim of this book is to showcase the natural beauty of the Hills and mention some of the qualities that make them so special.

The Shropshire Hills are well known for the astonishing variety of their landscape. They are unique in Britain in having such varied geology in a relatively small area, with rocks ranging from about 600 million years old to those that were formed in the last Ice Age a few thousand years ago. The earliest rocks were laid down 60° south of the equator near the Antarctic Circle, and have travelled a staggering 12,000 miles through the tropics over a period of 500 million years to reach their present position. As a result the Hills have a classic place in geological circles, and geologists come from all over the country to study them.

The archaeology of the Shropshire Hills is no less interesting. The earliest man-made structures that survive in the Hills belong to the Bronze Age spanning the period 2500–700BC, and include the ancient Portway track and tumuli on the Long Mynd and burial cairns on The Stiperstones. However, the most spectacular monuments from pre-history are the Iron Age hill forts, of which there are more than twenty in the Hills. These impressive monuments, with their massive ramparts and ditches, are usually sited on hilltops or ridge ends and dominate the surrounding landscape. Many show signs of permanent habitation.

Not surprisingly, given the diversity of the landscape, the Shropshire Hills provide a rich habitat for fauna and flora. This includes upland heath on the Long Mynd and The Stiperstones – home to upland birds such as grouse, wheatears and meadow pipits; deciduous and coniferous woodland where badgers, foxes and owls abound; and open grassland providing food and cover for farmland birds such as lapwings and skylarks. The flora includes heather, bilberry and bracken on the heathland, some rare wildflowers in the upland hay meadows, and a fine collection of orchids and other wildflowers on Wenlock Edge.

This book starts with a tour of the Long Mynd – the centrepiece of the Shropshire Hills – crosses the Stretton Valley to visit the rugged volcanic rocks of the Stretton Hills, goes north to climb The Wrekin, then circles around to explore The Stiperstones, the Clun Hills, the Clee Hills and finally, the famous limestone escarpment of Wenlock Edge.

I would like to thank Dr Ian Dormor, Shropshire Hills AONB Landscape Officer, geologist Dr Peter Toghill and Peter Carty, National Trust Property Manager for the Shropshire Hills for their help with this book, and above all my wife Alexandra for her unfailing support and patience.

Robin Jukes-Hughes, 2009

THE SHROPSHIRE HILLS
AREA OF OUTSTANDING NATURAL BEAUTY

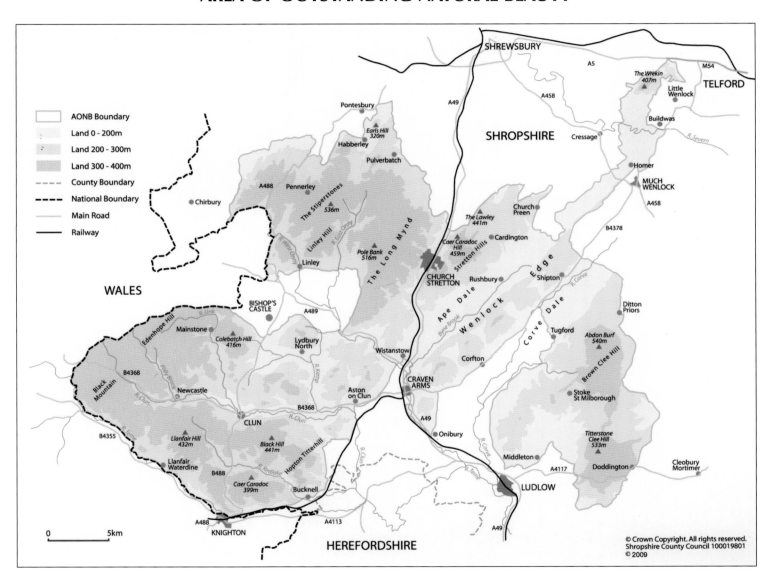

Legend:
- AONB Boundary
- Land 0 - 200m
- Land 200 - 300m
- Land 300 - 400m
- County Boundary
- National Boundary
- Main Road
- Railway

SHREWSBURY

The Wrekin 407m

Little Wenlock

TELFORD

M54

A5

A458

SHROPSHIRE

Cressage

R. Severn

Buildwas

Pontesbury

A49

Homer

MUCH WENLOCK

Earls Hill 320m

Habberley

Pulverbatch

A458

Church Preen

B4378

A488

Pennerley

The Lawley 441m

Cardington

The Stiperstones 536m

Linley Hill

R. East Onny

The Long Mynd

Caer Caradoc Hill 459m

Stretton Hills

Rushbury

Shipton

R. Corve

Chirbury

Pole Bank 516m

Linley

CHURCH STRETTON

Wenlock Edge

Ditton Priors

WALES

R. West Onny

BISHOP'S CASTLE

A489

Ape Dale

Corve Dale

Tugford

Abdon Burf 540m

Edenhope Hill

R. Unk

Mainstone

Colebatch Hill 416m

Lydbury North

Byne Brook

Brown Clee Hill

B4368

R. Kemp

Wistanstow

Corfton

Stoke St Milborough

Black Mountain

R. Clun

Newcastle

B4368

Aston on Clun

CRAVEN ARMS

A49

Tipperstone Clee Hill 533m

B4355

CLUN

R. Clun

Llanfair Hill 432m

Black Hill 441m

Hopton Titterhill

Onibury

Middleton

A4117

Doddington

Cleobury Mortimer

Llanfair Waterdine

B488

R. Redlake

Caer Caradoc 399m

Bucknell

R. Clun

R. Teme

R. Corve

LUDLOW

A488

KNIGHTON

A4113

A49

HEREFORDSHIRE

0   5km

The Long Mynd and Church Stretton from Caer Caradoc

THE LONG MYND

The Long Mynd was born 560 million years ago close to the Antarctic Circle. The sedimentary rocks were laid down in layers, a bit like the pages of a book. Earth movements folded them on their side on their journey north, so that the rock strata are now almost vertical across the Mynd from east to west. Ice and water have smoothed the plateau, leaving a steep scarp on the Welsh side and deeply cut valleys known locally as batches or hollows in the Stretton Valley. A Neolithic trade route known as the Portway runs along the spine of the Mynd from north to south and a number of Bronze Age burial mounds have been found along it. An Iron Age hill fort on Bodbury Hill overlooks Carding Mill Valley.

The Mynd first became popular as a tourist destination in the 1860s when it was advertised as 'England's Little Switzerland'. The National Trust acquired 5000 acres of it in 1965 and established their offices, shop and restaurant in Carding Mill Valley a few years later. They maintain a network of hiking trails and bridleways across the Mynd, and manage the heathland as a habitat for birds and wildlife. The National Trust also runs a thriving educational programme for about 24,000 children annually, mainly from the urban West Midlands.

Jonathan's Rock
Looking down the Batch Valley from Jonathan's Rock. Legend has it that a drover called
Jonathan used to meet his lady here, and flung himself to his death one day when she failed to turn up.

The Batch Valley in Autumn
Autumn colours are at their most intense shortly after dawn on a cold morning, but they
seldom last like this for more than a few minutes. Jonathan's Rock can just be seen on the skyline.

Gathering in the Sheep
Commoners have grazed their sheep on the Long Mynd since medieval times.
A farmer and his dogs are gathering in the sheep in Cwmdale for the annual shearing.

A Frosty Dawn in Cwmdale
Cwmdale is a secret valley hidden away from the Stretton Valley, and was once the site of a Saxon pen. The impressive hill on the far side of the Stretton Valley is Caer Caradoc.

Bodbury Ring Iron Age Hill Fort
The hill fort on Bodbury Hill dates from about 400BC and there is evidence
that it was permanently inhabited. The hill in the background is The Wrekin.

Ridge and Furrow Cultivation
The 'Ridge and Furrow' cultivation patterns below Bodbury Hill can best be seen on
a frosty morning while the sun is still low over the horizon.

Carding Mill Valley from the Air
An aerial view of Carding Mill Valley with the Long Mynd plateau beyond.
The steep road snaking up the hill on the left is The Burway. The National Trust offices,
shop and restaurant are in the red-roofed buildings in the foreground.

Carding Mill Valley from Bodbury Ring
Looking down into Carding Mill Valley from the
3m deep ditch on the north side of the hill fort.

Carding Mill Valley in Spring
The valley in spring, with a hawthorn tree in blossom in the foreground.
The outcrop of rock on the left is called Junction Rock.

Carding Mill Valley in Autumn

Carding Mill Valley in Winter.
A bird's eye view of the valley in winter. The ridge on the left of the
picture is called Cow Ridge and the hill in the centre is Calf Ridge.

17

Junction Rock
Junction Rock is a massive outcrop of hard Haddon Hill Grit, and is a Geological Site of Special Scientific Interest.
Drill cores taken along the base showed that the rocks were formed 60° south of the equator.

Carding Mill Valley from the Reservoir Path
There is a well marked trail from the car park in Carding Mill Valley to where the valley divides below Calf Ridge.
The Reservoir Path runs around the side of Cow Ridge to New Pool Reservoir and back to the car park.

New Pool Reservoir
This reservoir was built in Edwardian times and provided pure spring water
to the people of Church Stretton until the early 1960s.

Dr Mott's Road
Taking the right hand fork at the base of Calf Ridge leads to Dr Mott's Road – so named because a local GP had this path built so that he could use it to visit his patients on the other side of the Mynd. This is the easiest route from Carding Mill Valley up onto the plateau.

Light Spout Hollow
The left hand fork leads up Light Spout Hollow. The footpath up this valley is steep and narrow.

Approaching the Waterfall
The valley opens out on approaching Light Spout Waterfall.
The rare Ring Ouzel used to nest every year in these rocks,
but hasn't returned since 2004.

Light Spout Waterfall
This is the only waterfall of any size in the Shropshire Hills.
The fall is impressive after rain, but hardly merits the
title of 'England's Little Niagara' by which it was
advertised on Victorian railway posters.

Dawn on the Burway
A pre-dawn shot from Burway Hill looking towards Caer Caradoc.
The rocks on the right of the picture are known as Devil's Mouth Rocks.

Heather on Burway Hill
In recent years the heather on the lower slopes of the Mynd has been badly affected by Heather Beetles.
Warm winters and climate change are taking their toll on the fauna and flora of the Mynd.

Upper Townbrook Hollow
Townbrook Hollow is the next valley south from Carding Mill and a popular walk from
Church Stretton. The rock strata on Devil's Mouth Rocks are almost vertical.

Opposite:
Townbrook Hollow and Rectory Wood
The footpath down Townbrook Hollow with the gorse in full flower. Rectory Wood lies
at the bottom of the valley, with the small market town of Church Stretton beyond it.

Bluebells in Rectory Wood
Rectory Wood is a countryside park adjoining Church Stretton, and has
a fine display of snowdrops, daffodils and bluebells in springtime.

Wild Garlic in Hopes Wood
Hopes Wood adjoins Rectory Wood on the lower slopes of
the Long Mynd and is awash with Wild Garlic in May.

Ashes Hollow in Spring
Ashes Hollow near Little Stretton is perhaps the most beautiful valley in the Long Mynd.

Upper Ashes Hollow
Upper Ashes Hollow is a great area for bird-watching.
Peregrine falcons, merlins and ravens can all be seen here.

Ashes Hollow from the Long Mynd Plateau
Looking down Ashes Hollow from the Long Mynd Plateau below Pole Bank.
The round hill in the centre of the picture is Grindle Hill. The Clee Hills can just be seen above it.

Pole Bank from Pole Cottage
Pole Bank is the highest point on the Long Mynd at 516 metres above sea level.

The Pond at Pole Cottage
Several ponds behind Pole Cottage were made for duck shooting in the last century.
They are now great places for dragonflies and nesting wildfowl.

Wildmoor Pool
Wildmoor Pool is the largest of the 64 pools on the Long Mynd. Teal nest here most years.

Snow on the Long Mynd
The Long Mynd from The Stiperstones. Fifty years ago the Mynd was covered in snow for six months of the year, and the golf club was known as the 'six month club'. Snow is now a rarity and seldom lasts more than a few days.

The Long Mynd from Helmeth Hill
The Long Mynd from Helmeth Hill, with Church Stretton in the valley.

Above:
Common Buzzard
The buzzard is the iconic bird of the Shropshire Hills and can often be seen soaring high in the sky uttering its wild mewing cry. Rabbits form its main diet, but it also feeds on small mammals and carrion.

Top left:
Monarch of the Mynd
Sheep have grazed on the Mynd for hundreds of years. Their numbers have been greatly reduced in recent years under an agreement between the farmers and the government to safeguard the fragile heathland.

Left:
A Long Mynd Foal
A very small Welsh Mountain Pony foal, dwarfed by the reeds behind it. These ponies are thought to have been descended from Welsh pit ponies.

The Stretton Hills and Village of All Stretton from the Long Mynd

THE STRETTON HILLS

The Stretton Hills lie across the Stretton Valley from the Long Mynd on the other side of the well known Church Stretton Fault. This fault lies roughly along the tree line at the base of the Stretton Hills, and separates the sedimentary rocks of the Long Mynd to the west from the volcanic rocks of the Stretton Hills and The Wrekin to the east. Two tectonic plates clashed along this line millions of years ago, and it was once the scene of furious volcanic activity. Today it lies dormant, but a mini earthquake every ten years or so – enough to rattle the plates on kitchen shelves – reminds us of its origins.

The Stretton Hills stretch from The Ragleth in the south to The Lawley in the north. They are quite different in character from the Long Mynd, being long, narrow and steep-sided, and without heather cover. The volcanic rock from which they were formed lies close to the surface, and if you pick up a stone on the summit you will more than likely find that it is full of tiny holes – left when the lava cooled. Caer Caradoc, the highest of the Stretton Hills, is crowned by a fine Iron Age hill fort.

Frost on The Ragleth
The Ragleth rises above the village of Little Stretton, and has a fine ridge walk along its crest. The hill on the left is Hope Bowdler Hill, and the long ridge of Wenlock Edge can be seen on the skyline.

Snow on the Gaerstones
The Gaerstone is a magnificent crag of volcanic Rhyolite rock at the south end of
Hope Bowdler Hill and is a familiar landmark overlooking the small market town of Church Stretton.

Mist on the Stretton Hills
Mist rolling over the Stretton Hills at dawn. This photograph was taken from The Ragleth
looking north towards Caer Caradoc. The Wrekin can just be made out in the distance.

Morning Mist in the Stretton Valley
A view from Bodbury Hill across the Stretton Valley towards Caer Caradoc, with
Hope Bowdler Hill on the right. The 'Ridge and Furrow' cultivation below Bodbury Hill
can be seen on the golf course in the bottom right of the picture.

Wenlock Edge from Hope Bowdler Hill

This image was taken from just below the Gaerstone looking down Hope Bowdler Hill and across Apedale towards Wenlock Edge. The ridge walk along Hope Bowdler Hill is one of the finest but least known in Shropshire.

Caer Caradoc from Helmeth Hill

An autumn view of Caer Caradoc from Helmeth Hill, with Helmeth Wood in the bottom left of the picture. The main hiking trail from Church Stretton can be seen snaking up the flank of the hill.

Helmeth Wood from Helmeth Lake
A view of Helmeth Wood across the lake near New House Farm. Helmeth Wood
is owned and cared for by the Woodland Trust and is a haven for wildlife and wildflowers.

Bluebells in Helmeth Wood
Helmeth Wood is one of the best places for bluebells in the Shropshire Hills.

An Aerial View of Caer Caradoc
Caer Caradoc is the highest of the Stretton Hills at 459m high. The fine Iron Age hill fort
has three ditches on the north side, and a single entrance on the south side. It was once
thought to be the site of the last stand of the British King Caractacus against the
Romans in AD 50, but modern historians think this unlikely.

The Lawley from Caer Caradoc
Looking across the innermost ditch of Caer Caradoc hill fort towards The Lawley with
The Wrekin in the distance. Small terraces and building platforms within the hill fort
indicate that it was probably permanently inhabited.

Caer Caradoc from Inwood
A view of Caer Caradoc in springtime from the hamlet of Inwood near All Stretton.
Hawthorn trees are in full blossom in every hedgerow.

Caer Caradoc from the East
An unusual view of Caer Caradoc taken from a spur at the base of Willstone Hill.

Caer Caradoc in Winter
It is easy to see why the Victorians called this area 'England's Little Switzerland'.

Caer Caradoc from Little Caradoc
Caer Caradoc at dawn from the bump of Little Caradoc.

Foxgloves on The Lawley
This magnificent display of foxgloves could be seen from the Long Mynd, several miles away.

The Lawley from the Air
For a lovely ridge walk with magnificent views over the surrounding countryside, one can park near
Comley Farm in the bottom centre of the picture, walk up and along the 2 mile ridge from south to north,
and return along the public footpath which follows the line of the hedge at the base the hill.

The Lawley from Inwood
An autumn view of The Lawley looking across the Stretton Valley from the hamlet of Inwood.

The Lawley from Plush Hill
Plush Hill is a popular area for walking and riding, and has
wonderful panoramic views of the Stretton Hills and Valley.

The Lawley from Blackhurst
This view of The Lawley was taken in winter from the east side of the hill.

Mimulus, Coppice Leasowes Local Nature Reserve
Church Stretton is fortunate in having three nature reserves within its boundaries.
Rectory Wood and Helmeth Wood have already been mentioned. The third,
Coppice Leasowes, is owned and maintained by Church Stretton Town Council, and has a
wetland area on the west side of the A49 where Mimulus and Yellow Flag Iris abound.

Primrose Wood
Primrose Wood is also in Coppice Leasowes Local Nature Reserve, and lies on the east side of the A49 trunk road.
In a good year it has a wonderful display of Wood Anemones, Primroses and Celandines.

Snowdrops in Hough's Coppice
Hough's Coppice lies below Caer Caradoc, which can be seen in the backgound with snow still on its flanks.
Although privately owned, the wood adjoins a public footpath leading from All Stretton to Caer Caradoc.

The Wrekin from Cressage

THE WREKIN

The Wrekin rises sharply out of the Severn Valley to 405m and is the first hill to greet you as you enter Shropshire from the flat West Midlands plain. It is Shropshire's most famous hill, with a long history dating back to the days of the ancient Britons. The Iron Age hill fort on its summit is believed to have been the headquarters of the pre-Roman Cornovii tribe. The two ditches around it follow the contours of the hill, and there are traces of foundations of about 25 round houses within it. The fort was captured by the Romans in AD49, who subsequently built the town of Viriconium in its shadow – which in its time became the fourth largest town in Roman Britain.

The Wrekin was never an active volcano, but like the Stretton Hills it was formed from the debris of volcanic action about 560 million years ago. Another explanation for its formation dates from the days of giants. A wicked giant from Wales had a grudge against Shrewsbury and wanted to flood it by damming the River Severn. On his way there he met a cobbler and asked him how far he had to go. The wily cobbler was carrying a sack full of shoes to mend, and told the giant that he'd just come from Shrewsbury and it was so far that he'd worn out all the shoes on the way. The giant was tired and decided to dump his rocks where he stood, and so made The Wrekin.

The Wrekin from Haughmond Hill
A view from Haughmond Hill looking across the village of Uppington. Haughmond Hill is owned by the
Forestry Commission and has some lovely marked trails which are popular with the people of Shrewsbury and their dogs.

The Wrekin from the Severn Flood Plain
The River Severn in flood with The Wrekin beyond, with one of many
Second World War pillboxes which still guard this part of Shropshire.

The Wrekin from Little Hill Farm
Little Hill Farm lies below the hill of that name on the south west side of The Wrekin.
A small herd of inquisitive bullocks came to investigate the camera.

The Wrekin from Buckatree
This reservoir formerly supplied water to the town of Wellington. It is now a popular fishing lake.

The Wrekin from the North
This image was taken in early summer just off the road from Wellington to Little Wenlock.

April Showers on The Wrekin
Another image taken in early summer, this time from the
hamlet of Rushton on the west side of The Wrekin.

Oilseed Rape around The Wrekin
The fields surrounding The Wrekin are carpeted with oilseed rape in
May and June, and make a fine sight from the summit.

The Wrekin Path in Springtime
The main path up The Wrekin starts by the car park at Forest Glen on the Little Wenlock road and rises through glorious beech woods. The best time of day to climb it is shortly after dawn.

Approaching Half Way House
The path continues through beech woods to Half Way House, where you can get a warm welcome and a bite to eat.

Approaching Hell Gate
The path opens out above Half Way and becomes an easy stroll up to the summit. Hell Gate is the
north east entrance through the outer defences of the hill fort, and is angled to make it more difficult to attack.

Heaven Gate
The gateway through the inner line of defences is Heaven Gate. The foundations of the guard house
can be traced just inside the entrance. The head of a Roman javelin was found there in the last century.

The South West Gate
The South West Gate guards the inner line of defences at the south-west end of the hill fort.

A Raven in Flight
Ravens were almost extinct in England at the turn of the twentieth century,
but are now fairly common in the Shropshire Hills. This image shows off
their massive 4 ft wing span, heavy beak and V-shaped tail.

The Raven's Bowl
The bowl is said to have been formed when two giants were fighting on top of The Wrekin. One was pecked in the eye by a raven and shed a mighty tear in a bowl in the rock. It has always held water since.

The Needle's Eye
One of the fighting giants struck at the other with his spade.
He missed, and the spade descended to the ground and cleft the solid rock to form the eye.

The Eye of the Needle
It was said that a maiden would never marry her man if she looked back when passing through the eye. The cleft was blocked by a large pyramid-shaped boulder during an earthquake in May 1990.

The Wrekin from Lyth Hill
Lyth Hill is a countryside park just south of Shrewsbury, which is owned and maintained by Shropshire Council.
It has stunning panoramic views of the Shropshire Hills and is a popular recreational area for Shrewsbury people.

The Stiperstones Ridge

THE STIPERSTONES

The Stiperstones is a spectacular 10km long ridge, crowned by rugged tors of white quartzite. It lies just inside the border between England and Wales, and has stunning views from the ridge towards the Welsh mountains and the Shropshire Hills. Its rocks were formed around 480 million years ago during the Ordovician period. Severe frost during the last ice age broke up the quartzite to give The Stiperstones its unique formation today. It was declared a National Nature Reserve in 1982 because of its geology, landscape and wildlife, and its wild dramatic scenery.

Much of The Stiperstones is covered by heathland. Natural England who manage the Reserve, have a project called 'Back to the Purple' which aims to conserve and regenerate the heather cover along the whole length of the ridge. The heathland supports a wide variety of endangered flora and fauna. Grouse, curlew, and meadow pipits all breed on the ridge, and whinchats and stonechats breed on the edge of it. Buzzards and ravens are often seen and heard overhead.

Looking South from Manstone Rock
Looking down the ridgeline from Manstone Rock, with Cranberry Rock at the end of the ridge. Nipstone Rock, Black Rhadley Hill and Heath Mynd to the south of The Stiperstones are included in the 'Back to the Purple' project.

Cranberry Rock
This photograph shows how the quartzite was broken up into blocks during the last Ice Age. Walking boots are needed on The Stiperstones because the ground is so uneven. Broken ankles are said to average one a month!

Corndon from The Stiperstones in Winter
Corndon lies just over the border in Wales, but is a prominent landmark from many places in Shropshire.
The treacherous nature of the hiking trail can be seen in the foreground.

Corndon from The Stiperstones in Summer
The same scene in summer, with bell heather in bloom in the foreground.

Corndon on a Misty Dawn
A view of Corndon from further along The Stiperstones ridge.

Manstone Rock at Dawn

Manstone Rock in Summer
Manstone Rock is the highest point on The Stiperstones at 536m above sea level and the second highest in Shropshire. Local witches are said to gather here on the longest night of the year to elect their leader.

Climbers on Manstone Rock
Manstone Rock is a popular venue for budding rock climbers.

The Devil's Chair

It is said that the Devil sat down here when he was carrying a load of rocks to dam the River Severn. When he got up again his apron broke and his rocks made The Stiperstones.

The Devil's Chair from the North

Local people avoid the Chair when it is shrouded in mist, in case the Devil is sitting there.

A Hard Frost on The Stiperstones
This image was taken at dawn on a very cold January morning. The temperature
on The Stiperstones is usually a few degrees colder than the surrounding area.

Snow on The Stiperstones
The sheep are still covered with snow after an early morning fall. The prominent tor on the skyline is Manstone Rock.

Clun Hills from The Stiperstones
This image was taken later the same day, looking south from The Stiperstones towards the Clun Hills.

Squilver
Squilver is a hamlet at the base of The Stiperstones that started life as an upland farm. It then became an adventure training centre, and is now private housing. Residents are sometimes marooned for days after a heavy snowfall.

The Stiperstones from the Long Mynd
A dawn image of The Stiperstones from Wildmoor. As its name implies Wildmoor is a very wild and sometimes boggy part of the Mynd. The rare hen harrier is a regular visitor.

Eastridge Wood from Westcott Hill
Eastridge Wood lies at the northern end of The Stiperstones ridge, and the Stomp Trail runs through it before dropping down to Habberley. This image was taken on a winter's morning with frost still lying in the valley.

Tankerville Mine
The lower slopes of The Stiperstones have been mined for lead since Roman times, and extraction only ceased in the 1950s. The nearby Snailbeach Mine, which is open to the public, was once the largest lead mine in Europe.

Black Rhadley from Linley Hill
Black Rhadley Hill lies just south of The Stiperstones and is included in the 'Back to the Purple' project.

95

Mountain Pansies
The jolly faces of Yellow Mountain Pansies in an upland
hay meadow on the west side of The Stiperstones.

An Upland Hay Meadow near Rigmoreoak
Natural England look after The Stiperstones National Nature Reserve from their offices at
Rigmoreoak just south of Pennerley. This is one of several upland hay meadows they manage in the area.

Bromlow Callow
Bromlow Callow lies just west of The Stiperstones and is a prominent landmark in the area.
It is said to have been planted as a beacon to guide Welsh sheep drovers on their way to London.

The Clun Hills and Valley

THE CLUN HILLS

The Clun Hills are totally different in character to the rugged hills we have visited so far – being gentle rolling country, reminiscent of the downland in the south of England. The big hills to the east of Clun, like Hopton Titterhill, Black Hill and Bucknell Hill, are clothed with serried ranks of Forestry Commission spruces. Those to the west of Clun, known oddly as Clun Forest, are open grassland with barely a tree to be seen. The valleys are peaceful too, and sparsely populated with villages made famous by A.E.Housman in his lines 'Clunton and Clunbury, Clungunford and Clun, are the quietest places under the sun'.

Life was not always so peaceful in the Clun Hills – as witnessed by the proliferation of defensive works through the ages. They include three fine Iron Age hill forts at Burrow Hill, Bury Ditches and Caer Caradoc just south of Clun. The highest and best section of Offa's Dyke – the 168 mile long dyke along the Welsh border built by King Offa around AD790 – cuts through the hills east of Clun, and there are ruined Norman castles at Clun and Hopton Castle which saw bloody fighting in the Civil War.

Hopesay Common looking North
Hopesay Common is owned by the National Trust and has magnificent views of the Clun Hills
and Valley. This photograph was taken looking north up Caudibrook Valley with the Long Mynd in the distance.
The farmstead on the left of the picture is called The Fish, possibly because of some Christian connection.

The Clun Valley from Hopesay Common
A lovely view from the southern end of Hopesay Common
looking across the Clun Valley to Clunbury Hill.

Burrow Hill from Hopesay Common
Burrow Hill is crowned with a large Iron Age hill fort, much of which
is concealed by trees. A herd of moorland ponies grazes on the common.

Ditch at Burrow Hill Fort
The hill fort is fortified with two massive ditches and has a single entrance.
The inner ditch has been cleared and has good views to the valley below.

Bury Ditches Hill Fort

Bury Ditches was planted with conifers after the last war and the hill fort lay forgotten beneath them. A violent storm in 1976 felled many of the trees on the hilltop to reveal one of the finest iron age hill forts in the country. The Forestry Commission have since cleared the area and provided footpaths and information boards for visitors.

Massive Ramparts at Bury Ditches Hill Fort
The hill fort has up to five massive ramparts on the west side where the approach is less steep,
reducing to two on the steep eastern side. There are complex entrances at either end of the fort.

The River Redlake at Chapel Lawn
The River Redlake rises in the Clun Forest near Llanfair Hill, and flows through the attractive village of Chapel Lawn before joining the River Clun near Leintwardine.

Hodre Hill from Caer Caradoc
Hodre Hill is the only deciduous wood of any size in the Clun Hills.
This view was taken from the lower slopes of Caer Caradoc, south of Clun.

The West Entrance to Caer Caradoc Hill Fort
The hill fort on the other Caer Caradoc above Chapel Lawn is a perfectly symmetrical lozenge shape with angled entrances at either end. The bank at this entrance is armoured with rock and 7m high at this point – all dug by hand!

The View from the East Entrance
Looking down the Redlake Valley from the east entrance of the hill fort towards Hopton Titterhill and Bucknell Hill.

The Upper Redlake Valley from Caer Caradoc
Looking up the beautiful Redlake Valley towards Llanfair Hill on the skyline.

Offa's Dyke on Llanfair Hill
Offa's Dyke runs from the Dee Estuary in the north to the Severn/Wye confluence in the south, and reaches its highest point on Llanfair Hill at 430m above sea level. The dyke is also at its greatest depth at this point.

Abandoned Plough
An abandoned plough alongside Offa's Dyke between Spoad Hill and Llanfair Hill.

Offa's Dyke on Spoad Hill
Offa's Dyke on Spoad Hill above Newcastle-on-Clun.
The rolling grassland is typical of the terrain in the Clun Forest.

Red Kite
The red kite was last recorded nesting in Shropshire in 1876, and became extinct in England by 1900. It retained a foothold in a remote part of Wales, from which it has slowly spread out across Wales and into England. Two pairs returned to Shropshire to nest in the Upper Clun Valley in 2005, and the number of nesting pairs in the Hills is slowly increasing.

Clun Castle
Clun Castle rises above the village of Clun and stands guard over the Clun Valley. Originally a motte and bailey, it was rebuilt in stone around 1140AD and has been the site of many battles.

The Old Packhorse Bridge at Clun
The lovely old packhorse bridge at Clun dates from 1450 and remains largely unchanged.
Its piers have recesses in which pedestrians can take refuge from the speeding traffic.

Brown Clee from the Giant's Chair, Titterstone Clee

THE CLEE HILLS

The Clee Hills are the highest, most remote and least visited of all the Shropshire Hills – so remote that until the early part of the twentieth century they had their own dialect which was barely understood by people in neighbouring towns. They are remote even today, and a journey to the foot of Brown Clee involves negotiating many miles of single track lanes. Yet a visit is well worth the effort. The hills themselves are not spectacular, but the climbs are easy and the views from the summits of both Brown Clee and Titterstone Clee are stupendous. There is no higher ground to the east until the Ural Mountains in Russia.

The Hills were formed on the equator in the Carboniferous period about 300 million years ago, and comprise coal measures intruded by a sheet of very hard dolerite, known locally as Dhustone. They have been inhabited for centuries; there is a Bronze Age complex on Hoar Edge, four Iron Age hill forts on the summits and deserted medieval villages on the lower slopes. The hills have been mined for coal, iron ore and lime since Roman times, and until coal mining ceased in 1926 were the highest coalfields in the country. They have been quarried for Dhustone since 1860 and there is still a quarry in operation above Cleehill village.

Sunrise over the Clee Hills
A view of Brown Clee Hill from The Ragleth. The hill has two summits Abdon Burf
on the left, which is the highest point in Shropshire at 540m above sea level, and
Clee Burf on the right. Big Wood can be seen on the skyline between them.

117

The Clee Hills from The Ragleth
A pre-dawn image of the hills, with Brown Clee on the left and Titterstone Clee on the right.

Brown Clee from Millichope
Looking across the beautiful Corvedale Valley from the country estate at Millichope.

Ludlow and Titterstone Clee
The classic view across Ludlow, with Ludlow Castle in the left foreground,
and the great parish church of St Laurence towering above the town.

Titterstone Clee from Bitterley Church
Bitterley is an old mining village with a beautiful church dating back to the fourteenth century. There is a fine medieval cross in its churchyard. Coal mining on Titterstone Clee was first recorded in 1235.

Titterstone Clee from Dhustone
The village of Dhustone was built during the latter half of the nineteenth century to accommodate
the influx of quarrymen from all over the country who came to work in the new quarries.

Quarry Buildings on Titterstone Clee

Quarrying started in earnest on Titterstone Clee in 1860 and the stone was used initially for the construction of Cardiff Docks. The industry expanded considerably during the Victorian era to meet the enormous demand for stone for road and rail construction. At its height the industry employed 2000 men and produced 400,000 tons of stone annually.

Disused Quarry on Titterstone Clee
This small flooded quarry on the east side of Titterstone Clee produced high quality stone for setts.

View from the Hill Fort on Titterstone Clee
The Iron Age hill fort on Titterstone Clee covers 28 Hectares and is one of the largest in England. It was surrounded by a single rampart, most of which has been destroyed by quarrying. There are two Bronze Age ring cairns within it.

Abdon Burf from Nordy Bank Hill Fort
Nordy Bank Hill Fort lies on a spur below Clee Burf and is the only one of the four Iron Age
forts on the Clee Hills which has not been destroyed by quarrying. It is roughly oval in
shape and is well defended by a single rampart up to 3m high in places.

Titterstone Clee from Clee Burf
The distinctive shape of Titterstone Clee can be seen on the skyline about 4 miles away.

Iron Age Rampart on Clee Burf
This is the only section of the rampart around Clee Burf which has not been destroyed by quarrying.
Some huge quarry structures remain inside the perimeter. Big Wood is on the left of the picture.

RAF Memorial on Brown Clee
This memorial stone in front of Big Wood commemorates the twenty three Allied and German
airmen who died in air accidents on Brown Clee during the Second World War.
Their names, dates and aircraft details are recorded on the back.

Above:

The Summit of Abdon Burf

The summit of Abdon Burf, seen from in front of the RAF Memorial. The summit has been mined and quarried through the ages, and there is little trace of the Iron Age hill fort which once encircled it. The view from the summit is stunning.

Left:

Peregrine Falcon

Peregrine falcons were first recorded nesting in Shropshire in 1987. A pair nested in a disused quarry on Titterstone Clee in 1995 and have nested there almost every year since. Peregrines were almost wiped out by persecution and pesticides during the mid twentieth century, but they are now recovering well.

Clee Burf from the Summit of Abdon Burf
Looking back from Abdon Burf towards Clee Burf, with Titterstone Clee and its radome just visible on the skyline.

Apedale and Wenlock Edge from Sharp Stones

WENLOCK EDGE

'On Wenlock Edge the wood's in trouble .... the gale, it plies the saplings double' wrote A. E. Housman

Wenlock Edge is a 19 mile long escarpment of pure limestone formed about 400m years ago just south of the equator during the Silurian period. The two sides of the ridge are quite different: the north side being a steep escarpment clothed in thick woodland, while the south side is gently sloping farmland. It is famous for its fossil reefs that are similar to those being laid down in the Caribbean today. Indeed, its geology is so unique that rocks of the same type are referred to as 'Wenlockian' the world over.

Nearly half of the Edge, as it is known locally, is owned by the National Trust who look after the woodland and maintain more than 12 miles of excellent footpaths. Wildlife includes a small herd of fallow deer, three species of owls and a pair of peregrine falcons which nest most years in a disused quarry. At least twelve species of wild orchids grow on the limestone-rich soil.

Apedale from Ippikin's Rock
The view from Ippikin's Rock opposite the Wenlock Edge Inn. Ippikin was leader
of a band of robbers who had a hideout in a cave beneath the rock. The cave was
said to have been sealed by an earthquake leaving Ippikin and his band imprisoned forever.

Eaton under Heywood
Eaton under Heywood is a tiny hamlet on the north side of the Edge, with a manor house, a farm and a few
scattered houses, yet it has a fine twelfth-century church with some of the oldest yew trees in Shropshire in its churchyard.

Wilderhope Manor
Wilderhope Manor is a fine Elizabethan manor house on the south side of the Edge.
It was once owned by Major Smallman who famously leapt over the Edge on his horse when
pursued by Roundheads, landed in a bush – and survived. It is now owned by the National Trust
and used as a youth hostel. The manor house is open to the public on Sunday afternoons throughout the year.

Wenlock Edge from Longville in the Dale
An evening shot in autumn. The dale referred to in the
name is Apedale on the northern side of the Edge.

Wenlock Edge from Lushcott
Another autumn shot taken later the same evening.
The Wrekin can be seen between the trees on the left.

Old Quarry House, Blakeway Hollow
The disused Ballstone Quarry site at Blakeway Hollow is now maintained by the National Trust as a limestone meadow.
Wenlock Edge has been quarried for limestone for centuries, but quarrying operations have now ceased.

Pyramidal Orchids, Blakeway Hollow
Blakeway Hollow is rich in wildflowers, including
this wonderful display of Pyramidal Orchids.

Tawny Owl
Walk through the woods on Wenlock Edge on a summer evening and you are sure to hear the hooting of a tawny owl. It is the commonest of the three owls that are found on the Edge; the others being the barn owl and little owl.

Common Spotted Orchid
On Roman Bank. This orchid appears
sporadically along the length of the Edge.

Northern Marsh Orchid
On Roman Bank. This orchid can be
identified by its square flower head
and the vivid purple of its flowers.

Greater Butterfly Orchid
In Blakeway Coppice. This orchid
has a strong sweet scent which
attracts moths and butterflies.

Broad Leaved Helleborine
In Blakeway Coppice. This stunning
orchid grows up to 90cm in height
and may have up to 100 flowers.

Pyramidal Orchid
Above Lea Quarry. This is probably the
commonest wild orchid on Wenlock Edge.

Bee Orchid
Above Lea Quarry. Possibly the
most beautiful of all our wildflowers.

Corvedale from Wenlock Edge
A lovely view across Corvedale from Wenlock Edge.
Titterstone Clee can be seen on the skyline.